SAMURAI PRESIDENT
OF THE PHILIPPINES

SPIRITUAL INTERVIEW WITH THE GUARDIAN SPIRIT OF

RODRIGO
DUTERTE

RYUHO OKAWA
HS Press

Contents

Preface 7

4

10 Underground Plans for a New Worldview

11 After the Spiritual Interview from the Guardian Spirit of Duterte

This book is the transcript of spiritual interview with the guardian spirit of Rodrigo Duterte. The interview was conducted in English until the middle of Section 8, where it switched to Japanese. The rest of the interview is an English translation.

These spiritual messages were channeled through Ryuho Okawa by his extraordinary spiritual power. The opinions of the spirits do not necessarily reflect those of Happy Science Group. For the mechanism behind spiritual messages, see end section.

Preface

Recently, the Philippines President Duterte visited Japan. What kind of a person is he? Even the Japanese government, the mass media, and the scholars of international politics don't work effectively. If we don't know the mindset of Mr. Duterte, Japan cannot establish a clear decision on national security, and will always be under the control of American government.

The messages from the guardian spirit of President Duterte in this book is quite clear. Because this is a spiritual reading on him. His appearance is like an old-fashioned "Father," but his true entity seems to be the "Japanese samurai spirit." Japan should be strongly determined to trust the Philippine government, without much prejudice on his sayings (and acts) only.

He wishes for Japan's true independence. I hope readers to be excited about the discovery of a true (samurai) patriot.

Nov. 3, 2016
Master and CEO of Happy Science Group
Ryuho Okawa

Rodrigo Duterte (1945 - Present)

A Filipino politician. Born in Leyte. Upon graduating from the Lyceum of the Philippines University's Political Science Department, he passed his bar examination and became a public prosecutor. Since 1988, he served as the mayor of Davao for a total of seven terms over 22 years, improving the safety and economic conditions of the city. He took office as the 16th president of the Philippines in Jun. 2016. As a person who makes extreme remarks, he has been called the "Filipino Donald Trump." Duterte has used strong measures to crack down on narcotics and has executed one thousand several hundred suspects in several months via the police. In Oct. 2016, he visited Japan to hold a summit with Prime Minister Abe and agreed to solve the issue of the South China Sea peacefully under the rule of law. They agreed to a total and maximum yen loan of 21.4 billion yen (approx. 207 million USD).

Interviewers from Happy Science*:

Yuki Oikawa
Director of Foreign Affairs
Happiness Realization Party

Toshihisa Sakakibara
Executive Director
Director General of International El Cantare-Belief
Promotion Division

Jiro Ayaori
Managing Director
Chief Editor of *The Liberty*
Lecturer of Happy Science University

---

* Interviewers are listed in the order that they appear in the transcript. The professional titles represent the position at the time of the interview.

1
Looking through the Mind
Of the Mysterious President Duterte

RYUHO OKAWA

Good afternoon, everyone. This is my first contact. So, I cannot guarantee whether we can succeed or not, he is a good man or a bad man, I don't know. His god is an evil spirit or not, I don't know. He is gentle or not, I don't know. And in addition to that, it's very difficult to understand Tagalog English*, so [*to Sakakibara*†] you, transfer Tagalog English [*audience laugh*].

Sometimes his English could be read as Chinese or Spanish or like that. But in reality, it's English, so it's very difficult for me. But I can't speak Tagalog English correctly, so please forgive me about that. But I will try my best. I have not examined what he said, his guardian spirit says, what language his guardian spirit says, so it's English or Japanese or another language, I don't know.

So, in reality, this is the first contact. But I think he is very mysterious and just one or two days ago, he left Japan. We know only about the fact that he had a conversation

---

* Tagalog and English are the official languages of the Philippines. Their English has a Tagalog accent to it.

† Sakakibara, who is one of the interviewers, has experience as a branch manager at a Happy Science branch in the Philippines.

with Xi Jinping in China and in Tokyo, Mr. Abe or other people [see Figure 1]. And we are much troubled with his different opinion about China or the United States. So, today's main aim is, "What kind of a person is he?" No one knows correctly. Of course, Philippine people know a lot about him, but we, Japanese, cannot understand him correctly. And of course, people in the United States don't know him well.

But we have some kind of impression that he can be some kind of troublesome figure in the Asian district. So,

Figure 1.
President Duterte had talks with Chinese President Xi Jinping in Beijing on Oct. 20, 2016. While agreeing to a promise of approximately 2.5 trillion yen (approx. 24.2 billion USD) in economic cooperation, he shelved the issue of Chinese sovereignty over the South China Sea. Duterte then returned home before visiting Japan. He and Prime Minister Abe met (photo) and agreed on the supplying of two Japanese large-scale patrol boats and five billion yen loan (approx. 48.5 million USD), among other things, on Oct. 26. In regards to the issue of the South China Sea, President Duterte claimed that he thinks of the situation as similar to Japan's and that he intends to always stand by Japan.

is he a friend of China or a friend of Japan or a friend of the United States? Or, is he just thinking about his country only? We must look through his mind and make up our plan on how to deal with or cooperate with Philippine people or country or this president.

It's up to you, so I rely on you. But if some accident happens, at that time, please change your mind and settle the battle or some misleading conversation. I hope so. If it's difficult for you to speak in Tagalog English, you can use Japanese. I can understand and I will transfer the contents to him. He will say some kind of language at that time. OK, then, we'll try.

We will invite Mr. Rodrigo Duterte, the guardian spirit of Mr. President of the Philippines, Mr. Duterte, the guardian spirit of Mr. Duterte, would you come down here and answer our questions? Mr. Duterte, the guardian spirit of Mr. Du...

2

Impression of the Visit to Japan And of Prime Minister Abe

The guardian spirit somehow knows About Japanese Shinto

DUTERTE'S GUARDIAN SPIRIT

Uhn. Ahhhh. A-ha, ha.

YUKI OIKAWA

Mr. President. [*Duterte's G.S. suddenly gets out of his chair and takes off his suit.*] [*Audience laugh.*] Hello? Hello, Mr. President? Hello. Let me confirm. Are you the guardian spirit of President Duterte?

DUTERTE'S G.S.

What is a guardian spirit? Uh?

OIKAWA

OK. So, you are President Duterte?

DUTERTE'S G.S.

Duterte, Duterte, ah, yeah.

OIKAWA

OK. OK, yeah. It's a big honor having this session today here with you.

DUTERTE'S G.S.

Owner? Owner? What's owner?

OIKAWA

It's our pleasure. It's our big...

DUTERTE'S G.S.

Ah, *honor.* Uh? Honor, honor, honor, honor, honor, honor, OK.

OIKAWA

Thank you very much for coming today. And especially...

DUTERTE'S G.S.

Who are you? Who are you?

OIKAWA

We are Happy Science.

DUTERTE'S G.S.

What's that?

OIKAWA

We are Happy Science.

DUTERTE'S G.S.

What's that?

OIKAWA

The biggest Japanese spiritual group.

DUTERTE'S G.S.

Really? Really?

OIKAWA

Yes.

DUTERTE'S G.S.

No, no. *Ise-jingu* is the greatest.

OIKAWA

You are talking about Shintoism, right?

DUTERTE'S G.S.

Bigger. Bigger.

TOSHIHISA SAKAKIBARA

Japanese Shintoism. Yeah, we are different.

DUTERTE'S G.S.
Different?

SAKAKIBARA
Yeah, a new religion in Japan.

DUTERTE'S G.S.
[*Looking at Sakakibara.*] Oh, you are Filipino.

[*Audience laugh.*]

SAKAKIBARA
Yeah, I almost look like a Filipino, but I'm actually Japanese.

DUTERTE'S G.S.
Really? Oh.

SAKAKIBARA
But I used to live in the Philippines for two years. So, I'm very familiar with the Philippines. I'm very happy to see you, finally.

DUTERTE'S G.S.
Really? Uh, I think so.

SAKAKIBARA
Yes.

Feeling very sorry about missing the meeting with The "god emperor" of Japan

OIKAWA

Thank you, thank you for coming. So, first of all, you've just been to Japan and I know you have been here before to Japan, but this time it's official, right?

DUTERTE'S G.S.

Ah, you, speak slowly. Your English is not correct. OK?

OIKAWA

OK. I will speak slowly.

DUTERTE'S G.S.

Slowly. Correctly.

OIKAWA

OK. You have been to Japan, right?

DUTERTE'S G.S.

Yeah.

OIKAWA

Then, what was your impression of your visit this week?

DUTERTE'S G.S.

Uhn, uhn, I wanted to meet emperor, emperor, god emperor.

OIKAWA

Sorry for the cancellation of that session.

DUTERTE'S G.S.

Very sorry. I kill someone.

SAKAKIBARA

How did you feel about that? So, you missed...

DUTERTE'S G.S.

About that?

SAKAKIBARA

Yeah. You missed the opportunity to meet the emperor of Japan.

DUTERTE'S G.S.

Hmm... It means the emperor of Japan was very afraid of meeting with me because I am the greatest god of the Philippines, so that's the reason.

The one word to describe
Prime Minister Abe

OIKAWA

OK, what was your impression meeting with Mr. Abe?

DUTERTE'S G.S.

Abe.

OIKAWA

Mr. Abe.

DUTERTE'S G.S.

Abe. *Kechi* (Stingy) Abe.

OIKAWA

[*Laughs.*]

[*Audience laugh.*]

DUTERTE'S G.S.

Kechi Abe, kechi Abe, kechi Abe. Abe, Abe kechi, haha. Kechi, you know?

JIRO AYAORI

Do you want...

DUTERTE'S G.S.

Kechi is English, ah, you know?

OIKAWA

No.

DUTERTE'S G.S.

Oh...

AYAORI

Do you want more support from Japan?

DUTERTE'S G.S.

Ah... You know the amount China gave me, you know?

AYAORI

Yes.

DUTERTE'S G.S.

Hmm... Two, hmm... two thousand five hundred billion yen (approx. 24.2 billion USD) they gave me?

AYAORI

Hmm...

DUTERTE'S G.S.

Japan, five billion yen (approx. 48.5 million USD)[*]? Hmm? What is... huh, huh? Explain to me...

OIKAWA

So, you expected more money from Japan, right?

DUTERTE'S G.S.

Of course, of course. Japan should com... Oh, more competition, need more competition with China and must win China.

SAKAKIBARA

That's your real intention toward China, right?

DUTERTE'S G.S.

Hmm... Kechi, Abe kechi, kechi Abe, Abe kechi, Abe...

SAKAKIBARA

We'll talk to him.

---

[*] The yen loan is approximately five billion yen in funds but, in addition, Japan will construct two large-scale patrol vessels and deliver them to the Philippines after completion. Japan will offer approximately 16.4 billion yen (approx. 159 million USD) in loans as construction cost.

DUTERTE'S G.S.

Abe kechi *de*, Abe kechi. Uncle of emperor of Japan die[*] because of kechi Abe.

SAKAKIBARA

[*Laughs.*] I see. OK.

OIKAWA

OK. We're asking you about China later...

DUTERTE'S G.S.

I...slowly, slowly.

OIKAWA

[*Laughs.*] Slowly, OK.

DUTERTE'S G.S.

Correct English is very slow.

OIKAWA

All right, all right.

DUTERTE'S G.S.

You know?

---

[*] On Oct. 27, 2016, His Imperial Highness Prince Takahito Mikasanomiya, uncle to the current emperor, had passed away due to heart failure.

3
"Just Kill Bad People"

The "open secret" of his success as mayor

OIKAWA
So, your hometown is Davao in Mindanao, and you are the former mayor of Davao, right?

DUTERTE'S G.S.
Mayor, hmm...

OIKAWA
And during your time, Davao changed and became very prosperous, and became...

DUTERTE'S G.S.
Prosper...

OIKAWA
Yeah. And became...

DUTERTE'S G.S.
Good. Good, good. Sounds good.

OIKAWA

And very safe.

DUTERTE'S G.S.

Safe... Hmm...

OIKAWA

Right? So, I think...

DUTERTE'S G.S.

Safe, safer, safest.

OIKAWA

Yes. I think you are very good at doing economic policies. So, what was your secret?

DUTERTE'S G.S.

Secret? Just kill bad people[*].

[*Audience laugh.*]

DUTERTE'S G.S.

That's the secret. Not a secret. It's an open secret.

---

[*] Since President Duterte's assumption in office, he has been cracking down on drug crimes and has accepted "extra-legal murders" in which the police and neighborhood watchers execute suspects without trial. It is said that there have been over 2,000 suspects executed in this drug war, but his approval ratings from the citizens remain high.

OIKAWA

[*Laughs.*] Open secret.

"You need to pull off the bad tooth"

SAKAKIBARA

Yeah. Your way is kind of extreme.

DUTERTE'S G.S.

Oh... Your Tagalog English is not so correct.

[*Audience laugh.*]

SAKAKIBARA

[*Laughs.*] I'm very sorry. Your way to kill people to make peace is kind of extreme.

DUTERTE'S G.S.

Huh?

SAKAKIBARA

Extreme. But...

DUTERTE'S G.S.

Are you speaking English?

SAKAKIBARA
[*Laughs.*] Yeah.

DUTERTE'S G.S.
Really?

SAKAKIBARA
[*Laughs.*] Sorry.

DUTERTE'S G.S.
Uh-huh.

SAKAKIBARA
People in the Philippines are very happy, especially in Davao.

DUTERTE'S G.S.
Uh-huh.

SAKAKIBARA
And I heard about you a lot that you were a very good mayor in Davao, and improved a lot of things. So...

DUTERTE'S G.S.
Good is not enough.

SAKAKIBARA

Excellent.

DUTERTE'S G.S.

Capable or excellent.

SAKAKIBARA

Most excellent mayor in the Philippines.

DUTERTE'S G.S.

Yeah. Most talented.

SAKAKIBARA

So, we'd like to know about you more because you are a kind of a mysterious person for us...

DUTERTE'S G.S.

Uh-huh.

SAKAKIBARA

...For the people not only in Japan, but also in the world. So, could you tell us about your basic philosophy or belief? How you...

DUTERTE'S G.S.

Basic philosophy?

SAKAKIBARA
Yes. How you founded the way to...

DUTERTE'S G.S.
Where are you from? From Greek?

SAKAKIBARA
Ah, me?

DUTERTE'S G.S.
Uh.

[*Audience laugh.*]

SAKAKIBARA
I'm Japanese.

DUTERTE'S G.S.
Oh... Japanese, OK. Philosophy?

SAKAKIBARA
Philosophy or belief in yourself.

DUTERTE'S G.S.
Kill people. Bad people.

SAKAKIBARA

[*Laughs.*] So, how did you reach that way of thinking in order to make peace or bring peace? Why did you reach that kind of belief to bring peace, to kill the people is the best way?

DUTERTE'S G.S.

Umm. When your tooth hurts, you need a *penchi* (pliers) and pull off the bad tooth. It's the only way to solve your...

Same answer when asked about The future vision of the Philippines

AYAORI

So, what is your vision of the future Philippines?

DUTERTE'S G.S.

Pigeon? Pigeon? Pigeon is good for French (cuisine)...

AYAORI

French?

DUTERTE'S G.S.

French? Pigeon, pigeon. You like pigeon?

AYAORI
No, sorry.

DUTERTE'S G.S.
No?

AYAORI
Your *vision.*

DUTERTE'S G.S.
Vision?

AYAORI
Future Philippines...

DUTERTE'S G.S.
Vision...vision...vision...

OIKAWA
Future. Your future image of your country.

DUTERTE'S G.S.
To kill bad people completely. Last one or he come to police or kill the last one. Like *Gokiburi* (cockroach). No? Ban, ban, ban!

OIKAWA

OK, you mean bad people are maybe doing drugs...

DUTERTE'S G.S.

And I'm the Batman of Philippines.

OIKAWA

Batman. OK. So, I think you are targeting the drug addicts.

DUTERTE'S G.S.

We have four million people.

OIKAWA

Drug addicts?

DUTERTE'S G.S.

Yeah, yeah, yeah.

OIKAWA

Right. So, you are going to...

DUTERTE'S G.S.

I must kill all of them but if they convert their hearts to God, I will give them forgiveness.

OIKAWA

Yes, but drug business is dominated by China. So, your country receives so many drugs from China. So, if you really solve this problem...

DUTERTE'S G.S.

And people of our country sell drugs to Japan, Japanese people, Japanese Yakuza. So, I am working for Japan in reality.

OIKAWA

You're going to fight against China's drug industry?

DUTERTE'S G.S.

China's drug? Your English is very difficult. China's drug? Fight with China's drug? China's yakuza? China's drug? China's bad people? Criminal?

OIKAWA

I mean China is sending many drugs to the Philippines.

DUTERTE'S G.S.

No, no, no, no, no. We are producing drugs in our country. China is an importer from us.

4

How Does He See America and Japan As the God of the Philippines?

Officially a Catholic, but who is his God?

SAKAKIBARA
May I ask your religious belief?

DUTERTE'S G.S.
Religious belief?

SAKAKIBARA
Because you have that kind of a belief...

DUTERTE'S G.S.
I am a person of mercy.

SAKAKIBARA
Mercy? OK. Where does that thought come from?

DUTERTE'S G.S.
Come from?

SAKAKIBARA
Yes. I heard the rumor that you are a Muslim believer. No?
Or a Christian?

DUTERTE'S G.S.
Maybe I am a... I am the god of Philippines, so is this
Muslim or Catholic, I don't know. But I am a god. I'm a
god.

OIKAWA
Officially, you are Catholic.

DUTERTE'S G.S.
Officially, yes.

OIKAWA
But maybe not. Are you Muslim?

DUTERTE'S G.S.
No.

OIKAWA
Who is your God?

DUTERTE'S G.S.
My God? Oh, I am God.

OIKAWA

You are? You are God?

DUTERTE'S G.S.

Yes.

The truth about the voice of God
He heard on the airplane

SAKAKIBARA

But recently when you arrived to Davao City and you had an interview with the reporters, you answered...

DUTERTE'S G.S.

Reporter. Reporter, reporter...pronounce correctly. *Reporter.* OK?

SAKAKIBARA

Sorry, my poor pronunciation. But, so your answer to the reporters was that you heard God's calling[*]. Ah, the God's calling that...

---

[*] Upon his return from Japan on Oct. 27, President Duterte held a press conference to announce that he would refrain from using harsh language, the reason being that he had received a calling from God.

DUTERTE'S G.S.
God is meaning me.

SAKAKIBARA
You, yourself?

DUTERTE'S G.S.
Me, me. Yeah.

SAKAKIBARA
But you said, superficially, that you have received the message from God. And then, the God said that if you continue to speak ill of others very badly, He would let the airplane go down. So, what is the meaning of that message or who is the God you are talking to?

DUTERTE'S G.S.
Almighty God.

SAKAKIBARA
Almighty God? OK.

DUTERTE'S G.S.
I swear I'll never say Mr. Barack Obama is a son of prostitute before I kill him.

SAKAKIBARA

[*Laughs.*] Before you...

AYAORI

So, did you send that message to Mr. Duterte?

DUTERTE'S G.S.

Huh?

AYAORI

In the prayer?

DUTERTE'S G.S.

Yeah, we are one.

AYAORI

Did you say that?

DUTERTE'S G.S.

I'm a god and he's god's son.

SAKAKIBARA

Actually, Mr. Duterte received the message from the guardian spirit of himself. OK? That's the meaning.

DUTERTE'S G.S.

Yeah. He is the only son of god. The god is me. OK?

SAKAKIBARA

OK. OK.

His connection to Typhoon Haiyan
That attacked the Philippines

OIKAWA

OK. OK. You talked about the god of the Philippines.

DUTERTE'S G.S.

Yeah.

OIKAWA

And in the past, 2013, we had a big typhoon which was called Haiyan.

DUTERTE'S G.S.

Oh, Haiyan.

OIKAWA

That time, we had this kind of spiritual interview right here and we realized... [See Figure 2.]

DUTERTE'S G.S.

Haiyan is my friend.

OIKAWA

Oh.

DUTERTE'S G.S.

He killed a lot of people instead of me killing people with gun.

OIKAWA

Haiyan said that Haiyan is the sea god of Philippines. So, he...

DUTERTE'S G.S.

Sea god? Then I'm the god of Heaven.

Figure 2.

On Nov. 12, 2013, Master Ryuho Okawa conducted a spiritual reading of Typhoon Haiyan that swept the Philippines. The spirit behind the spiritual cause of the typhoon identified itself as the god of the Philippines. See *Exploring the Spiritual Truth of the Massive Typhoon in the Philippines* (Tokyo: Happy Science, 2014).

OIKAWA

God of Heaven?

DUTERTE'S G.S.

Yeah.

SAKAKIBARA

Of the Philippines?

OIKAWA

I see. So, you know Haiyan very well?

DUTERTE'S G.S.

He or she, I don't know... It is a god of the Philippines Sea, around there. And I'm shining all over the world through Heaven, meaning sky.

OIKAWA

I see. That time, Haiyan insisted that the U.S. troops in the Philippines should leave the Philippines. And this time, you said the same thing.

DUTERTE'S G.S.

Yeah, it's true, it's true.

OIKAWA

So, you really want the U.S. troops to withdraw from the Philippines?

DUTERTE'S G.S.

They are intruders, so they need punishment from us. We are intruded by them. Japan, also. So, we are friends, Japan and...

OIKAWA

Ah, you mean, Japan and the Philippines are friends?

DUTERTE'S G.S.

Yeah, friends. We are intruded by bad America, so we are friends.

OIKAWA

Why America has to have punishment?

DUTERTE'S G.S.

Because they killed a lot of Philippine people. Tens of thousands of people.

OIKAWA

So, you are...

DUTERTE'S G.S.
Especially in Davao, around Davao, Mindanao.

"Japan had to kill MacArthur at that time"

OIKAWA
So, you are anti-white?

DUTERTE'S G.S.
White?

OIKAWA
White people.

DUTERTE'S G.S.
White people?

OIKAWA
The U.S. and western...

DUTERTE'S G.S.
You mean, stupid people? White in the brain?

OIKAWA
OK. From this perspective, if you look at the past history like World War II, which happened in Asian countries

including the Philippines, was especially the hot place that many people died.

DUTERTE'S G.S.

Uh-huh.

OIKAWA

So, how do you see World War II? What is your opinion?

DUTERTE'S G.S.

Oh... Japan's victory is a great one. Japan nearly escaped with the victory. Japanese army should have killed General MacArthur* at that time. That's the point.

OIKAWA

I see. Yeah, we really agree. So, we believe that the war was an Asian independent revolution from the White countries. Do you agree?

DUTERTE'S G.S.

Hmm... We were occupied by the U.S. at the end of 19th century. And Japan came to save Philippine people. That's

---

* Just after the outbreak of the Pacific War, the Japanese military aimed for the capture of the Philippines, which was then an American colony. The U.S. and the Philippine forces were forced to withdraw from Manila. Douglas MacArthur, who was the commander, left the Philippines in Mar. 1942, the year after the outbreak of the war, and fled for Australia.

a good work, good job! And General MacArthur ran away to Australia. He's not a samurai. He should *Seppuku* suicide at the time. He's not a samurai. He's bad, and in addition to that, he dropped the atomic bomb, Hiroshima and Nagasaki. They are Hitler-like people. Hmm.

5

The Guardian Spirit Reveals His True Thinking on China

"We need Japan to protect weak countries of Asia"

AYAORI
So, I'm wondering what is your opinion about Sino-Japanese War.

DUTERTE'S G.S.
Oh?

AYAORI
Chinese-Japanese War.

DUTERTE'S G.S.
Chinese-Japanese War?

AYAORI
Yes.

DUTERTE'S G.S.
You mean before *Daitoa Senso* [the Greater East Asia]War?

AYAORI
Yes.

DUTERTE'S G.S.
China and Japan?

AYAORI
Yes.

DUTERTE'S G.S.
Hmm...

AYAORI
What is your side?

DUTERTE'S G.S.
Japan came to China to save Manchuria. And Mao Tse-tung was a very coward person and he always ran away from Japanese army deep into the south part of China. He's a coward and he's not a hero. I cannot agree with his military award. It's just by chance he received his fruits. Japan should perish Chinese communist party.

AYAORI
Uh-huh.

DUTERTE'S G.S.
I think so. They are now growing bigger and bigger. And they are threatening us, Philippine people. We don't have

enough army to fight against them. So, we need Japanese help. But we hate American aids. They are intruders, so we hate America. So, Japan should stand up by herself and protect not only Japan, but also other weak countries of Asia. This is the Japanese destination.

OIKAWA
Including your country?

DUTERTE'S G.S.
Yeah, of course. Of course. It's Japan. Japan can, could kill General MacArthur.

The money from China is the Rental fee of South China Sea?

AYAORI
You mentioned that the Philippines relies on China. You said that.

DUTERTE'S G.S.
Yeah.

AYAORI
But that is not your true thought. Is it?

DUTERTE'S G.S.

They gave a lot of money, so...haha... I said so. But it is effective within my presidency. So, it's no more than 10 years. We got 2.5 *cho* [trillion] yen (approx. 24.2 billion USD), so it's great. More than half of our national budget*. So, it's our rental fee of our South China...

OIKAWA

South China Sea?

DUTERTE'S G.S.

Yeah, yeah, yeah, yeah. Rental fee. Rental. [*Laughs.*] So, it's good for 10 years.

AYAORI

But it will not be rental.

DUTERTE'S G.S.

Rental. Just rental.

AYAORI

No, I don't think so.

DUTERTE'S G.S.

After that, we'll attack them and get their buildings and their ships, of course, with the aid of Japan.

---

* The national budget of the Philippines was approximately 2 trillion pesos in 2013, 2.3 trillion pesos in 2014, and 2.6 trillion pesos in 2015. The exchange rate on November 1, 2016, was 1 PHP≈2.17 JPY.

SAKAKIBARA

When you met Xi Jinping the other day [see Figure 3], you were chewing a gum.

DUTERTE'S G.S.

Chewing a gum?

SAKAKIBARA

Yeah.

DUTERTE'S G.S.

Aaahhh!

SAKAKIBARA

So, what was your real intention in doing that?

Figure 3.
On October 20, 2016, President Duterte met with President Xi Jinping during his visit to Beijing.

DUTERTE'S G.S.

At that time, I don't know the reason but General MacArthur came to me and he advocated that "Please chew a gum and you'll look like General MacArthur." He said so. So, I pretended.

OIKAWA

What was your impression of Mr. Xi Jinping?

DUTERTE'S G.S.

He's a... he has poor mind and... Oh! Oh!! I cannot say bad things. So, he is bigger than I. It's great.

He is just dealing with China to get money

OIKAWA

But you don't like Chinese communist, do you?

DUTERTE'S G.S.

Huh?

OIKAWA

You don't like Chinese communist.

DUTERTE'S G.S.

Chinese communism...China has two faces. Superficially, they say that they have loyalty to communism but in reality, they have a habit of gathering money, day by day. It's a money-earning country, so in reality, it's a capitalism. They have two faces. We cannot believe in their political policy. So, we must have the same attitude. We must have respect to China. And another side, we must dis...dis...oh, bad words. By the way, we must respect Japan.

OIKAWA
OK.

DUTERTE'S G.S.
OK, OK, OK.

OIKAWA
So, you are so realistic that you are just dealing with China to get money, right?

DUTERTE'S G.S.
Oh, yeah, that's right. Yeah.

OIKAWA
So, you are not pro-Chinese.

DUTERTE'S G.S.
Huh?

OIKAWA
You are not pro-Chinese.

DUTERTE'S G.S.
Pro-Chinese? What? What English is that?

OIKAWA
You don't like China?

DUTERTE'S G.S.
Oh... my mother came from China, so...

OIKAWA
Mother's grandparents?

DUTERTE'S G.S.
Yeah, like that. So, I don't hate them. Only I ask them to give money. That's all.

OIKAWA
OK.

DUTERTE'S G.S.
It's just a Chinese main policy or Chinese mentality, hmm...to be Chinese means to love money more than life. It's Chinese, OK? To be Japanese means love money next to life. It's the difference.

OIKAWA
Very interesting.

SAKAKIBARA

So, Chinese people, especially the communist people, believe in materialism. And people in the Philippines don't like materialism because they believe in God. So...

DUTERTE'S G.S.

God, believe in God.

SAKAKIBARA

So, you will agree with people in the Philippines?

DUTERTE'S G.S.

Huh?

SAKAKIBARA

So, you have the same faith in God. So, you hate materialism?

DUTERTE'S G.S.

What do you mean by materialism? If you mean, materialism mean paper money and coin, we are materialism.

SAKAKIBARA

Ah, no, no. Materialism denies the existence of God.

DUTERTE'S G.S.

Ah, really?

SAKAKIBARA

Yeah.

DUTERTE'S G.S.

Materialism means bread and money or...

SAKAKIBARA

Because we need that for living. But basically, communist people don't believe in God.

DUTERTE'S G.S.

Oh... Why?

SAKAKIBARA

So, that's the problem.

DUTERTE'S G.S.

Ah... Because Xi Jinping is a replacement of God. Of course, Duterte is God, so almost the same. But Duterte is a God of Jesus Christ, so the situation is a little different.

"The United States and Great Britain should Apologize to Asian people"

SAKAKIBARA

OK. And so, while you express that you are supportive to China, on the other hand, you speak ill of Americans. The people are so afraid that American people will go away from the Philippines, especially business people and developers.

DUTERTE'S G.S.
Uh-huh.

SAKAKIBARA
Yeah. That means, in a sense, the economy in the Philippines will decline. That's what we are afraid of. So, what do you think about that?

DUTERTE'S G.S.
American people did nothing for the Philippines. It's the same as Okinawa. Okinawan people went mad because of American military forces. They are Japanese, but they are not Japanese. They are not Chinese, but they want to be Chinese. I understand. American policy changed people into becoming mad. Like the Great Britain changed India into very poor country and made them under human being. So they, both Great Britain and the United States, are very bad. They have been very bad. They should apologize to Asian people. Japan is the only savior for us and the last hope for us. So, I declared Mr. Abe, *bimbo* Abe, we are standing in the same side. We are friends.

SAKAKIBARA
I see.

6

His Outlook on the South China Sea Problem with China

Both the Philippines and Japan must cut the leash

AYAORI

So, in Beijing, you stated that the Philippines would break away from the U.S. What did you mean by that?

DUTERTE'S G.S.

I hate Obama.

AYAORI

Will you leave from the U.S. economically and militarily?

DUTERTE'S G.S.

Ah, it's recommendable policy. We must have our own independent policy. If we are not independent, we are not one nation, one country, we rely on Japan first, next China, and America is lower than third.

OIKAWA

So, let me confirm. Are you going to protect your country without U.S. troops?

DUTERTE'S G.S.

U.S. troops are occupying us. We are not a dog on leash, you know? Dog on leash. It's American policy. We must cut the chain, the leash. Japan also. Japan must become independent. Japan is a greater country than now. You are. So, we expect you and when the Chinese Xi Jinping gave us 250,000 billion yen (approx. 24.2 billion USD) to us, Japan must give 500 thousand billion yen (approx. 48.5 billion USD) to us. Twice. You understand? Go *cho-en* (approx. 48.5 billion USD). Go cho-en. You know? You know? It's Japanese amount. *Goju oku* (approx. 48.5 million USD)? No, no, no, *sukunai.*

OIKAWA

So, you expect much more money from Japan?

DUTERTE'S G.S.

It's *tetsuke* [deposit], tetsuke, tetsuke. You know?

OIKAWA

OK, OK. I have another question about the Philippines god. So, about 20 years ago, Mount Pinatubo had an eruption.

DUTERTE'S G.S.

Mount Pinatubo's eru...

OIKAWA

Mount Pinatubo's explosion. And that became the reason the U.S. army left the Philippines. So, do you have any relations with the Mount Pinatubo's explosion?

DUTERTE'S G.S.

[*Laughs.*] Ha, ha, ha. Oh, you go to hospital. [*Audience laugh.*] You should.

OIKAWA

Why?

DUTERTE'S G.S.

We are realistic. We are realistic, so we are not dreamers. We don't need any illusion.

OIKAWA

So, you didn't need the U.S. in the Philippines?

DUTERTE'S G.S.

Pinatubo. OK. Now just kill bad people and make a country for a good direction and become wealthy. And we, Japan, China should make a new colleague, colleague for Asia. A new EU for Asian people. It's good. America should go back to America.

He wants to improve the safety in the Philippines
And invite Japanese capitals

SAKAKIBARA

So, do you have any idea how you can solve the problem of the South China Sea?

DUTERTE'S G.S.

South China Sea? If we can get rental fee, it's OK.

SAKAKIBARA

OK, so you think it is the Philippines' territory originally?

DUTERTE'S G.S.

Originally.

SAKAKIBARA

And if China forcefully invaded and ruled that area, what would you do about it?

DUTERTE'S G.S.

But after I made a visit to Beijing, our fishing boat became safe. In addition to that, I borrowed two more big Japanese patrolling ships. It's to protect our fishing people from China, Chinese battleship or like that. So, I made it perfect.

SAKAKIBARA

I see.

OIKAWA

Did you talk about that with Mr. Abe?

DUTERTE'S G.S.

?

OIKAWA

Did you talk about what you said right now about the South China Sea problem with Mr. Abe?

DUTERTE'S G.S.

He just asked me, "Please understand our situation." He said it just like that. Mr. Abe was very afraid of having Barack Obama acknowledge the total amount of helping us, so he wanted to hide the amount. Under the table, he gave me a promise. It's more helpful for Filipinos to make a promise with Japan because it has a lot of money. We want to use more and more money every year. So, if I kill bad people in the Philippines and made a safe city, safe country, Japan can build a lot of factories and industries. And UNIQLO will come to the Philippines from China and we will make prosperity. Under the table we shook hands with Mr. Abe. Mr. Abe and Philippine president, yeah.

So, China is now expanding, but in reality, they don't have enough money. I know about that. Japan has real money, affluent money by Kuroda Nichigin General, so we can receive more money. We have...

OIKAWA

I see, I see. But you know, coming back to the South China Sea, if China successfully invades the Scarborough Reef, that would be a big problem, not only for your country, but also for Japan.

DUTERTE'S G.S.

No, no, no, no, no, we'll lose fishing rights. But they made a promise that they will buy our banana instead of fish. So, it's OK.

OIKAWA

Is it enough?

DUTERTE'S G.S.

Enough, enough, enough, enough.

"We don't need to protect our sea"

SAKAKIBARA

How about securing the route of oil?

DUTERTE'S G.S.
Hmm?

SAKAKIBARA
Yeah, oil. Importing the oil. So...

DUTERTE'S G.S.
Importing the oil.

SAKAKIBARA
That's...

DUTERTE'S G.S.
Japanese Self-Defense Army will be active in the near future, so it's OK. No problem. We'll support you.

AYAORI
At this point, it's not possible.

DUTERTE'S G.S.
Oh, really?

AYAORI
Yeah.

DUTERTE'S G.S.
It's OK, it's OK, it's OK.

AYAORI

Japan will not be able to deal with military conflict in the South China Sea so quickly.

DUTERTE'S G.S.

At that time, we'll buy coal from Australia, Mongolia district. And we have solar panel.

OIKAWA

So, the U.S. will leave your country and Japan cannot send our troops to your area. So, without the U.S. and Japan, how do you protect your sea?

DUTERTE'S G.S.

Ah, OK, OK. We don't need to protect our sea. We don't think it's a problem. Sea is not a problem. Problem is fish. Fish are swimming from China to the Philippines, Vietnam, Japan, all around the world. So, they cannot have nationality. Fish don't have nationality. So, we will do another... China has a great population, so they need fish, I understand. Japan also. But Japan has new technology for breeding fish artificially. So, we don't have much. It's OK. Around the Philippines, there are a lot of fish, so no problem.

SAKAKIBARA

So, you think like that because the Philippines is mainly dependent on the first stage industry. OK.

OIKAWA

So, you're really comfortable with the promise with China, so you allow to do the fishing?

DUTERTE'S G.S.

Because they gave us two-thirds of their national budget in my one visit. My second visit will be crucial for them. Hahaha!

AYAORI

But I think it's possible that China will invade your country. Not only the reef islands, but your main land will be intruded.

DUTERTE'S G.S.

At that time, I will be the president of China.

AYAORI

Oh, really?

DUTERTE'S G.S.

Because I can kill bad people. I'm stronger than Xi Jinping.

7

The Guardian Spirit's Vision
Of the Asian Century

He is "the god of mercy inviting inferno
For the United States"

SAKAKIBARA

So, where are your firm beliefs or thinking, to kill or punish to improve or bring peace, coming from? From your depths of your soul?

DUTERTE'S G.S.

Hmm...

SAKAKIBARA

So, you're the god of punishment?

DUTERTE'S G.S.

Ah, no, no. Mercy. Of course. God of mercy is inviting new inferno for the United States. They did bad things in these 100 years, so they need to apologize to Asian people. Of course, European people must apologize to African and Asian people or Indian people.

Next age will be the age of China and India. So, it means the age of Asia. And we have good friendship with

India and China. These two countries have almost half of the population of the world. So, next is the Asian century.

SAKAKIBARA

I see. Has it already been decided in Heaven that you were going to be the president of the Philippines?

DUTERTE'S G.S.

Huh?

SAKAKIBARA

In Heaven, has it already been decided or planned that you're going to be the president of the Philippines at this time? Is it God's plan?

DUTERTE'S G.S.

You know, I'm the Ironman and I'm the Batman of the American hero who descended to the Philippines. So, I'm a hero. Hero of the people. So, they supported me about 90 percent. You understand? 90 percent!

SAKAKIBARA

Yes, yes. I heard about that.

DUTERTE'S G.S.

Almost 90 percent.

SAKAKIBARA

Extraordinary rate.

DUTERTE'S G.S.

It's a God. Nearly equal to God.

OIKAWA

I understand that you are a hero. But you know, it seems your way of thinking is based on nationalism rather than globalism.

DUTERTE'S G.S.

Nationalism?

OIKAWA

Now, most of the world leaders are globalist.

DUTERTE'S G.S.

Globalist.

OIKAWA

For example, Obama is a globalist. But you are purely nationalist. So, that's a difference.

DUTERTE'S G.S.

I'm the president of the Philippines, so I must think, "Philippines first" like "American first."

OIKAWA

Philippines first?

DUTERTE'S G.S.

They think America first. We think Philippines first.

"Trump will let Japan go as an Asian leader"

AYAORI

In the U.S., presidential election is coming. What do you think about the candidate Mr. Trump and Mrs. Clinton?

DUTERTE'S G.S.

Mr. Trump says America first and Hillary will continue the next Obama, Obama the 2nd like that. So, Trump will be better because he will let Japan go as an Asian leader, so it will be helpful for us. Japan-Philippine relationship is very good. We are friends. We cannot break our promise. So, I rely on Japanese people.

American troops did bad things, but they never revealed that kind of bad deed and they condemn other countries only. Japan or Germany or Italy, like that. But they have their own intention to intrude us. They are at the opposite side of the Earth. They should not come to Asia.

Hawaii is not their country. They should give Hawaii to Japan. Japanese colony first, I think so.

OIKAWA

So, you don't like Obama, but you prefer Trump?

DUTERTE'S G.S.

Yeah. He's good. He just has concern about building new Trump Tower only, so it's good [*audience laugh*] for him and for us.

OIKAWA

OK. So, if Trump wins the election, do you think you can create a new relationship with the U.S.?

DUTERTE'S G.S.

No, no. We make new relationship with Japan, and Japan will remake the relationship with the U.S. It's enough.

Suggesting Japanese as the official language
Of the new Asian economic area

OIKAWA

Maybe Trump will say, "The U.S. armies should leave other countries." So, Japan, the Philippines, and NATO. Are you happy to do that?

DUTERTE'S G.S.

We have small power now, so we don't have enough political power to say. But for example, the United Nations secretary-general, it's a Korean secretary-general... who was that?

SAKAKIBARA

Ban Ki-Moon?

DUTERTE'S G.S.

Ban Ki-Moon. Stupid Ban Ki-Moon. Under the stupid Ban Ki-Moon, there can be expected nothing. So, it cannot be expected nothing. So, we ask Japan, "Have leadership in Asian area. We can rely on." But America is far from us, so they don't understand our situation. They think we are one of the islands of China or like that. They think like that. Obama especially doesn't understand the difference between Okinawa, Ishigaki, Senkaku, Taiwan, Scarborough Islands or around that, and Davao. He doesn't understand Davao.

SAKAKIBARA

I see.

DUTERTE'S G.S.

So, they are indifferent to us.

SAKAKIBARA

Yeah, of course. Yeah, I agree that America is far from Asia. But on the other hand, because of the American occupation in the Philippines, so many people are living in the United States doing their business. So, how do you care about those people in the United States?

DUTERTE'S G.S.

We are officially using English, but I think we should change our official language from English to Japanese. So, it's a greater future, I think. And China also must learn Japanese, it should be their official language. India also, use Japanese. Japanese trading area will have more than three or four billion people. It will make new economic area. We can survive.

SAKAKIBARA

We are happy to hear that.

OIKAWA

However, some of the Southeast Asian countries, like Cambodia, Laos, are going to China's zone, China's territory. What do you think about them?

DUTERTE'S G.S.

Hmm.

OIKAWA

We are afraid the Philippines will belong to China, like Cambodia and Laos.

DUTERTE'S G.S.

OK, OK, after that, Japanese army will occupy Beijing, so it's OK. No problem.

8
Revealing His Deep Connection To Japan and Speaking in Japanese

"I have a shrine in Japan"

SAKAKIBARA

So, you do like Japan and Japanese. Are you spiritually connected to Japan?

DUTERTE'S G.S.

Of course, of course, of course.

SAKAKIBARA

Could you tell us about?

DUTERTE'S G.S.

Hmm?

SAKAKIBARA

About more...

DUTERTE'S G.S.

More?

SAKAKIBARA

Yeah, your strong ties.

DUTERTE'S G.S.
Ah, I was Japanese.

SAKAKIBARA
Really?

DUTERTE'S G.S.
Uh-huh.

SAKAKIBARA
Could you tell us the name of your past life?

DUTERTE'S G.S.
Past life?

SAKAKIBARA
Yeah, in Japanese.

DUTERTE'S G.S.
Ah, I forgot, but I have a shrine in Japan.

SAKAKIBARA
Oh, wow.

AYAORI
Which era were you born in?

DUTERTE'S G.S.
Hmm?

AYAORI
Which *era*?

DUTERTE'S G.S.
Which *area*? Near here.

OIKAWA & AYAORI
Near here?

SAKAKIBARA
Near here?

DUTERTE'S G.S.
Un (Yeah).

OIKAWA
So, any related to the Philippines trade in the past Japanese history?

DUTERTE'S G.S.
No, I was a warrior of Japan or a general of Japan.

INTERVIEWERS
Oh.

AYAORI
In World War II?

DUTERTE'S G.S.
Hmm...

OIKAWA
Before World War II?

DUTERTE'S G.S.
Un.

A past life as a great general during Japan-China War and Japan-Russia War

OIKAWA
One of the famous Japanese soldiers?

DUTERTE'S G.S.
Un.

SAKAKIBARA
Admiral Togo?

DUTERTE'S G.S.
Admiral Togo? Oh, not so bad. It's OK *yo*. Un. Not so bad. Not so bad. Very akin to him.

SAKAKIBARA

Ah, akin to him.

AYAORI

In the Japanese-Russo War?

DUTERTE'S G.S.

Hmm?

SAKAKIBARA

Akin to him, ah, hmm.

OIKAWA

Which war in Japanese history did you join?

DUTERTE'S G.S.

Japan-China War, and Japan-Russia War.

AYAORI

Oh, General Nogi [see Figure 4]?

DUTERTE'S G.S.

Yeah.

AYAORI

Oh, it's great. I admire you.

DUTERTE'S G.S.

General Nogi is my past life.

[Hereafter, the interview was conducted in Japanese.]

OK, let's speak Japanese.

AYAORI

[Laughs.] *[Audience laugh.]* Oh, my... *[laughs.]*

Figure 4.

Maresuke Nogi (1849~1912) An officer from the Choshu feudal clan and a general in the Imperial Japanese Army. Participated in Kiheitai in the second Choshu conquest and fought against shogunate forces. After the Meiji Restoration, he went to the front of the Seinan War and the First Sino-Japanese War. He led the capture of Port Arthur as the commander of the Japanese Third Army in the Russo-Japanese War. He later became an education officer for Emperor Showa. On the day of the imperial funeral of Emperor Meiji, Nogi and his wife followed him to his grave. He is worshipped in Nogi Shrines all over Japan including the one in Akasaka of Minato Ward.

DUTERTE'S G.S.

I'm not good at English.

AYAORI

[*Laughs.*] [*Audience laugh.*]

DUTERTE'S G.S.

If I don't speak English, International Headquarters cannot get money. [*Audience laugh.*] So, I'm trying my best.

AYAORI

[*Laughs.*]

DUTERTE'S G.S.

It's too much. Japanese is OK. I want to say, "It's enough." [*Audience laugh.*] You know?

I'm mad at Japanese politics. Do you understand? [*To Ayaori.*] If I say in Japanese, you can do well. Come on. Let's make it the income of *The Liberty*[*].

AYAORI

[*Laughs.*] [*Audience laugh.*] Then, do you mean Japan...

DUTERTE'S G.S.

A god. A god, you know? It's not a lie, you know?

---

* A Happy Science magazine featuring opinions on politics, economy, etc. Ayaori is its chief editor.

AYAORI
You are right.

DUTERTE'S G.S.
Yeah, a god. I have a shrine. A god. Yeah.

9

Regain the Spirit of Meiji
And Stand up, Japan

He complains about the
Emperor's abdication problem

AYAORI

The thing you expect the most from Japan is military...

DUTERTE'S G.S.

Be independent. Independence! Yeah. I cannot forgive the corruption since Emperor Showa.

AYAORI

Corruption?

DUTERTE'S G.S.

Abdication of the Emperor*? I cannot forgive. It must be the end. The end of the Imperial Family.

---

* On Jul. 13, 2016, Japanese media outlets reported that His Imperial Majesty Akihito showed his intention to the Imperial Household Agency that he wished to abdicate the title, while alive, to the crown prince. On Aug. 8, the emperor's video message was broadcasted on television. Currently, regarding the legislation that will allow for early abdication, the government is discussing how they can establish special measures laws to accept early abdication for one generation without revising the Imperial House Act.

AYAORI

Ah, so you cannot forgive abdication?

DUTERTE'S G.S.

The Imperial Family will perish.

AYAORI

I see. Ah.

DUTERTE'S G.S.

So, I cannot forgive. No.

AYAORI

Do you mean that the abdication itself is not a good thing?

DUTERTE'S G.S.

It's not good. The Imperial Family will perish. Yeah, yeah. They will perish. They can do anything freely.

OIKAWA

They are trying to cover that by a special measures law, but is it not good?

DUTERTE'S G.S.

No, no, no. You know... Ah, I'm speaking Japanese. I guess it cannot be helped.

AYAORI

[*Laughs.*] [*Audience laugh.*]

DUTERTE'S G.S.

It cannot be helped because you found out.

You know, letting the emperor step down and Mr. Abe extends his term. It's unforgivable. I cannot forgive this kind of thing as a subject of the emperor. It's not good.

AYAORI

But this is the will of His Imperial Majesty.

DUTERTE'S G.S.

His will is not good.

AYAORI

Not good?

DUTERTE'S G.S.

He must not have his own will.

AYAORI

Ah, he must not have his own will?

DUTERTE'S G.S.

People above the clouds must not have a will.

AYAORI

Oh, oh.

DUTERTE'S G.S.

Yeah, yeah. I educated Emperor Showa so much. It's too sad.

OIKAWA

The present emperor repeatedly said "personal opinion," but it's not allowed?

DUTERTE'S G.S.

He must not say his opinion. It's a political opinion, you know? He is the fundamental character of Japan. He must not speak. He must not speak too much. It's not good at all. It will leave a risk for the next generation. Will the next one be the last or not? It depends.

AYAORI

Hmm.

DUTERTE'S G.S.

Hmm. It was revealed. And I was doing my best to speak in my poor English [*pounds table*] [*audience laugh*].

Ill words are "to teach the samurai spirit to Japan"

AYAORI

Time is almost up, but what are you expecting from Japan right now in particular?

DUTERTE'S G.S.

Please regain the Meiji spirit. Of course. Yeah! It's the only way. So, I came here all the way from the Philippines to Japan and I'm telling you to become strong. They are doing something stupid in Okinawa, so I came to say my opinion on behalf of you from the Philippines. To America, I said, "Obama, go to Hell." I spoke ill of him. So, I'm teaching the samurai spirit to the Japanese people...

AYAORI

I see. [*Laughs.*] So, that was a samurai. [*Laughs.*]

DUTERTE'S G.S.

..."You are much stronger." Than the Philippines. Even the Philippines can say something like that, so speak out more. I want to say so.

AYAORI

So, even if you receive a lot of money from China, which you said was a rental fee, ultimately, "Japan will solve the issue for us" is your true thought, right?

DUTERTE'S G.S.

You know, Japan will definitely stand up. You know, Japan is contained by America's "cap in the bottle"[*] logic, so you must remove it.

AYAORI

OK. Ah, yeah.

DUTERTE'S G.S.

You must definitely remove it. And establish religious value and protect by yourself. Also, contribute to the people of Asia. That is Japan's duty. Surely. You must turn that around. It was wrong after World War II, so you must return it to the original position. So, I'm supporting you from the Philippines now. So, you know...

OIKAWA

Does the spirit of Meiji period include religious policies?

DUTERTE'S G.S.

Yeah, of course.

You say I killed more than one thousand several hundred drug addicts or drug dealers, but do you know how many people were killed at 203 Hill[†]? I don't care about it at all.

---

[*] The way of thinking that symbolizes Japanese rearmament and militarization as "coming out of a bottle" and the U.S. forces in Japan as the "cap" that prevents them from doing so.

I will do anything for righteousness. First, I will improve the safety in the Philippines, and we can attract companies from overseas. No one will come to a dangerous place. Not at all.

And they are investing a lot into China, so we have to let them shift their investments next. In order to do that, we need to make a safe country in Southeast Asia. That's what I'm thinking right now. So, don't think badly of me. OK? Do you understand?

OIKAWA
I understood very well.

Suggesting the Greater East Asia Co-Prosperity Sphere To Japan from a foreign country

DUTERTE'S G.S.
OK? You understand that I'm a god. A small one, but a god. Surely.

AYAORI
There is something I want to ask you about. You said it would be OK with Mr. Trump, but it could be Ms. Hillary. Very likely.

---

† The Siege of Port Arthur during the Russo-Japanese War, where Maresuke Nogi served as the commander, saw casualties of about 60,000 Japanese and 46,000 Russian soldiers. Nogi himself lost two of his sons in this war.

DUTERTE'S G.S.

For now, yeah. If America wants to decline, then it's OK. It will decline. If Ms. Hillary wins, she will try to keep Japan and the Philippines on a leash like a dog, but America will get weaker, so in the end, the leash will come off. So, in the end, they will become independent. It's the same thing.

So, we must make the Asian region stronger. The EU will break up next. Yeah. So, we must make Asia stronger. We should control China and India well and create a prosperity area of Asia. The Greater East Asia Co-Prosperity Sphere is correct. It was the right thing. I'm trying one more time to make Japan create that. From us. You don't listen unless you are told from foreign countries. I'm thinking of doing it from this side. So, inform people well through *The Liberty*. OK?

AYAORI

OK.

DUTERTE'S G.S.

The Nogi Shrine is about to go down. It's about to be sold. It will be an apartment or something like that if it's left as it is.

Advice for the Happiness Realization Party And Happy Science

OIKAWA

Since this is a rare opportunity, could you give some words of advice for the Happiness Realization Party?

DUTERTE'S G.S.

Ah, you know, mountains of dead people. Wonderful.

OIKAWA

[*Smiles wryly.*]

DUTERTE'S G.S.

It's wonderful, I think. Wonderful. It's wonderful. You are showing Nogi spirit. It's good! Good!

Don't give up. If you do it for 10 years, the world will change. Yeah. Surely. The Japanese mass media cannot stand more than 10 years. They will treat you fairly. Definitely.

They cannot just keep reporting Liberal Democratic Party versus the alliance of opposition parties. They are just gathering without policies. You are insisting the right thing, so if the mass media keep ignoring you for 10 years, they are "no longer human." OK? Osamu Dazai*, you know? It's no good.

---

* Osamu Dazai (1909-1948) is a Japanese writer. The book, *No Longer Human* is one of his popular novels.

So, keep going for three more years. Then, there will be more fans. There will be more fans, definitely. Don't be discouraged. It's OK. The way will surely open. There is railroad in front of you. There is. Now, we are trying to make up for Japan's failure. We will do it.

OIKAWA

Thank you very much.

SAKAKIBARA

This is a rare chance, and there's Happy Science activities in the Philippines, too.

DUTERTE'S G.S.

Go, go. Do more. Jesus is just a servant. You know, he's just a servant or a manager. He's a manager, so use him more.

SAKAKIBARA

Umm, OK. [*Laughs.*] Do you have any advice? We are spreading our teachings in Asia, too.

DUTERTE'S G.S.

We want Japan to be more cool. Be cool. Show us the samurai spirit. Your indecisive attitude is miserable. Be a man and show us the heart of samurai! Then the Philippine people will be attracted! It must be like that. Japanese people must pull themselves together. I think so.

10
Underground Plans for
A New Worldview

"I will take as much as I can from China"

AYAORI

From what you said earlier, it sounded a bit cruel, but what's your vision for the Philippines besides killing bad people? [*Laughs.*]

DUTERTE'S G.S.

First, right morals should prevail in the Philippines. That's important. You need to raise the quality of people, or nothing can be built. If we don't raise the level of people and establish right morals, education will be meaningless. They will use it for bad things. We want to have good relations with Japan from now on and become more powerful. You are saying other Asian countries will be intruded by China, but it's in a bubble. I know that. I will take as much money as I can.

AYAORI

Oh, then, right now...

DUTERTE'S G.S.

Yeah. I will take as much as I can. I didn't make a real promise. I just got the aid first.

AYAORI

I see, I see.

DUTERTE'S G.S.

Yeah. I didn't say until when. It's like Islam. "As Allah wills."

Reformers will come from Asian countries based On the world plan by Happy Science

OIKAWA

So, then, are you aiming to become a great economic power?

DUTERTE'S G.S.

Yeah. But I'm not aiming just for the prosperity of one country. I'm thinking of making an Asian team. So, China just needs to change their system. No? Then, you can be better friends with them. Maybe. But don't be too weak before that. I think so. You need to stand firmly. It's not good for you to be chained by America.

So, you know, the UN? Their "winning countries" structure? It needs to break down. If not, there will be no resurrection of Japan. Yeah. So, the next move, I thought about it already. I thought about it well. We, for support, now, are in the neighbor countries. A reformer will appear from inside China.

AYAORI
Ah, really?

DUTERTE'S G.S.
Soon. Yeah. Coming.

AYAORI
Is that a part of your plan?

DUTERTE'S G.S.
We will show you. A reformer is coming soon. We will turn things around. Over there.

So, outside and inside, both need to act together. And Japan needs leaders who can do that. Now, we are accumulating our power in the field of thoughts. And we will turn things around. We will surely create a powerful prosperity area in Asia one more time.

AYAORI

OK. Also, a person who was Japanese in her past life but is Taiwanese in this life has become the president.*

DUTERTE'S G.S.

Right. So, we have a lot of underground plans. So, it's OK.

AYAORI

Taiwan and the Philippines...

DUTERTE'S G.S.

Thailand also. We will definitely, definitely, definitely change.

AYAORI

Who are the ones at the center of this plan? The Japanese Shinto gods?

DUTERTE'S G.S.

It's Happy Science! What are you saying?

AYAORI

Is that so? [*Smiles wryly.*] Hmm.

---

* On Feb. 7, 2016, Happy Science recorded a spiritual interview with the guardian spirit of Tsai Ing-wen, who won the Taiwanese presidential election on Jan. 16 by a landslide. In the interview, it was revealed that her past life was Chomin Nakae, who was also known as "the Rousseau of the East." See *Kinkyu Shugorei Interview Taiwan Shin Soto Sai Eibun no Mirai Senryaku* [Urgent Spiritual Interview with the Guardian Spirit of New Taiwanese President –Future Strategy of Tsai Ing-wen-] (Tokyo: IRH Press, 2016).

DUTERTE'S G.S.

Here is the center. Here is the center of the world! Uh-huh. We are born based on that plan. We predicted Japan would lose in World War II, so we chose to be born again to rebuild after it.

AYAORI

OK.

End the "winning countries" system of the UN and Make a new worldview

OIKAWA

Is that why you criticize the UN so much?

DUTERTE'S G.S.

The UN is bad. I cannot allow them to continue. It's wrong if they think that continuing their "winning countries" system is justice. They are wrong. Germany is not treated fairly also. They are being deprived of their money from the EU, but they are not allowed leadership. It's a very slave-like situation, just like Japan. We must free them. So, we must make a new worldview.

I can do just one part only, but at least I will end American hegemony and make China powerless at the same time. I will do those at the same time. Withdrawal of American hegemony and making China weaker. At the same time. Japan must become the leader of Asia. It's the only way. Japan should be the leader of Asia and Oceania.

Japan should regain the spirit of 1970s and 1980s. That's important. America is losing its mission now. We need the next mission, Asia mission. You, Happy Science, must carry that.

You are building the foundation now. Maybe you are not getting anything in return now, but the longer it takes, the bigger the fruit will be in the future. It's very huge. So, the EU will get weaker little by little, but Germany will still be its center.

Problems of the mass media in the Japanese Election system and in democracy

OIKAWA
You met with Mr. Abe this time. What was your real impression on him?

DUTERTE'S G.S.
No one else can replace him. [*Laughs.*] I guess so. It's sad. But there is a problem in the election system. The mass media are aiming to protect themselves. They want to keep

the status quo. They want to keep the status quo, so they are working hard to get closer to the administration.

I don't think this is the correct way of democracy. The emperor said he will hand over the position, but they reported it as abdication. There is a difference between handing over and abdication. Abdication means he might be expelled. Handing over means he will become a retired emperor.

AYAORI
True.

DUTERTE'S G.S.
So, the current emperor said he will hand over the position meaning that he will become a retired emperor. But the mass media keep saying abdication. They kept saying that and brainwashed all the people. So, he has no choice but to resign. The mass media report that it's his will, so even though he says something in protest, it will be a political opinion.

That's the point. I might kill 20,000 or 30,000 people, but please be tolerant and welcome me. Do you know how many people I got killed at 203 Hill?

AYAORI
[*Laughs.*]

DUTERTE'S G.S.

Maybe about 100,000. So many people died, but it was very important to win against Russia. That's how important it was. I don't want to lose what we did. Don't lose the prosperity, value systems, and culture of Japan that we worked hard to make, from the world. So, it's OK. Even if China tries to take in, it will be Japanized. The opposite will happen.

Heaven's plans to make China weaker

AYAORI

I think it would be very difficult to make China weaker...

DUTERTE'S G.S.

We will do it. We will. It's OK. There is no mistake with Heaven's plans.

AYAORI

Oh! I see.

DUTERTE'S G.S.

We have a detailed plan.

AYAORI

So, you mean, it has been taken care of in many ways?

DUTERTE'S G.S.

Yeah, it has been taken care of. It's OK. Just carry out what you need to do and succeed in it. This is important.

AYAORI

OK.

Comments on the Northern Territories Issue with Russia

OIKAWA

Mr. Abe will be meeting Mr. Putin in December, but what is your opinion on the issues with the Northern Territories?[*]

DUTERTE'S G.S.

Two islands will be returned if you negotiate. These two islands were a promise. Regarding the other two islands, you cannot get them back without a war. If not, you can get them back if Russia falls under a financial crisis, and asks us

---

[*] In Dec. 2016, President Putin will visit Japan to hold talks with Prime Minister Abe at his hometown in Yamaguchi Prefecture. Many believe this will be a big opportunity for the talks to push negotiations on the Northern Territories.

to buy them. Otherwise, the two islands won't come back. Tens of thousands of people are living on the islands.

Two islands will come back. Only around a thousand people live there. You can get them back if you negotiate well. Still, it's progress. I think it's better to make a peace treaty. So, it depends on the negotiation. If Putin and Trump can both do well with Japan and form a triangle, it will be good. Hmm.

"I am one of the founding gods of Japan"

AYAORI

Is this your first time being born in a foreign country?

DUTERTE'S G.S.

Hmm? No, I have been, but most of the time, I was born in Japan. It's been mainly Japan, yeah. I am definitely one of the founding gods of Japan.

AYAORI

Were you Masashige Kusunoki[*]?

---

[*] In a spiritual interview recorded in 2013, Maresuke Nogi referred to his past life by saying, "I was the one who said, 'Even If I were reborn seven times, I will protect this country.'" It is thought that he was Commander Masashige Kusunoki (1294?~1336), who vowed unfailing devotion to his country upon his suicide by sword. See Chapter 2 in *Akiyama Saneyuki no Nihon Bouei Ron* [Saneyuki Akiyama's Defense Theory of Japan] (Tokyo: Happy Realization Party, 2010).

DUTERTE'S G.S.

Yeah, maybe something like that.

AYAORI

Is there any other past lives you can tell us about?

DUTERTE'S G.S.

You don't know names other than the emperors. I was in ancient times, yeah.

AYAORI

Were you a helper of an emperor...

DUTERTE'S G.S.

I have helped during the time when the Imperial Household was established.

AYAORI

I see, I see.

OIKAWA

Thank you for your time, in both Japanese and English...

DUTERTE'S G.S.

Your English was difficult.

OIKAWA

I'm sorry [*laughs*].

DUTERTE'S G.S.

OK, OK.

OIKAWA

Thank you very much.

DUTERTE'S G.S.

So, I might be called a mad dog or something like that, but please support me and that I heard the voice of a god was not a lie.

Why does he pretend to be uncivilized unlike his Past life as a great general?

AYAORI

[*Laughs.*] So, are you just pretending to be uncivilized? You are not a rude person, originally.

DUTERTE'S G.S.

I get popular...

AYAORI

Oh, really [*laughs*] [*audience laugh*].

DUTERTE'S G.S.

...that way in the Philippines.

AYAORI

Oh, so you're doing it for the Filipinos.

DUTERTE'S G.S.

Hmm, well, like Schwarzenegger. Like him. That is what I'm doing. In a similar way, you know? There are a lot of crimes in the Philippines and the people are bad. I must tighten it.

AYAORI

I see.

DUTERTE'S G.S.

So, a scary person will appear...

OIKAWA

Isn't it about human rights or something?

DUTERTE'S G.S.

To be honest, I don't care about human rights at all because I am a god. It's OK, if final result is good. But the small, that Obama with small balls.

AYAORI & OIKAWA

[*Laughs.*]

DUTERTE'S G.S.

He doesn't have, in fact. I'm really angry with him. Hmm.

AYAORI

Yeah, I understand your true thoughts.

DUTERTE'S G.S.

You do? This is a big news for *The Liberty*.

AYAORI

Yeah, it's a really big scoop.

DUTERTE'S G.S.

So, half the income of this session goes to the International Headquarters [*audience laugh*]...

SAKAKIBARA

Thank you.

DUTERTE'S G.S.

Around half goes to *The Liberty*. It's just that...

AYAORI

Thank you.

DUTERTE'S G.S.

You must give back something.

OIKAWA

Thank you for your time today.

DUTERTE'S G.S.

Ah, OK, OK.

AYAORI

Thank you very much.

SAKAKIBARA

Thank you very much.

11

After the Spiritual Interview from The Guardian Spirit of Duterte

RYUHO OKAWA

[*Claps hands twice.*] I didn't expect this kind of conclusion. It is quite hard to disguise oneself.

AYAORI

But he was quite a noble person.

RYUHO OKAWA

He really was.

AYAORI

Quite a big difference...

RYUHO OKAWA

He was a prosecutor before. When people see him, they will think he is a gangster, for a moment.

AYAORI

[*Laughs.*] Yeah.

RYUHO OKAWA

But he was born into an upper class family in the Philippines and is the son of a lawyer, and became a prosecutor. So, he is just acting based on the rule of law. There is no death penalty in the Philippines. So, trials are meaningless, because drug dealers come back. And sometimes judges receive bribes and they become not guilty, so killing them seems to be most effective. Around his age, they were the ones that killed people, so that is why they can stand it. Japanese now don't have this kind of feeling.

It is not good to be too rude, but they are trying to tighten up. And since we are trying to become closer with Russia because Putin was Japanese [see Figure 5], we should

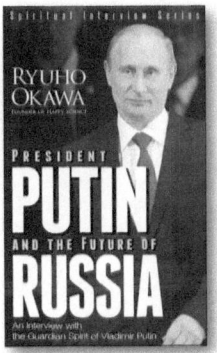 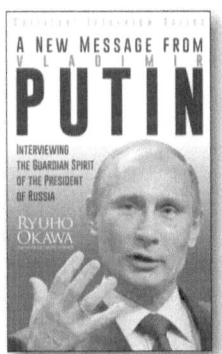

Figure 5.
In his previous spiritual interviews, it was revealed that President Putin's past lives consisted of Emperor Shomu who erected the Great Statue of Buddha in Nara, the eighth Muromachi Shogunate Yoshimasa Ashikaga, and the eighth Edo Shogunate Yoshimune Tokugawa. See *President Putin and the Future of Russia* (Tokyo: HS Press, 2012) and *A New Message from Vladimir Putin* (Tokyo: HS Press, 2014).

also have a friendly relationship with the Philippines. Now we know what kind of person he is.

This is a scoop. Yes. Thank you.

AYAORI

Thank you very much.

RYUHO OKAWA

The presidency is tough work.

ABOUT THE AUTHOR

Founder and CEO of Happy Science Group.

Ryuho Okawa was born on July 7th 1956, in Tokushima, Japan. After graduating from the University of Tokyo with a law degree, he joined a Tokyo-based trading house. While working at its New York headquarters, he studied international finance at the Graduate Center of the City University of New York. In 1981, he attained Great Enlightenment and became aware that he is El Cantare with a mission to bring salvation to all humankind.

In 1986, he established Happy Science. It now has members in over 166 countries across the world, with more than 700 branches and temples as well as 10,000 missionary houses around the world.

He has given over 3,450 lectures (of which more than 150 are in English) and published over 3,100 books (of which more than 600 are Spiritual Interview Series), and many are translated into 41 languages. Along with *The Laws of the Sun* and *The Laws Of Messiah*, many of the books have become best sellers or million sellers. To date, Happy Science has produced 26 movies. The original story and original concept were given by the Executive Producer Ryuho Okawa. He has also composed music and written lyrics of over 450 pieces.

Moreover, he is the Founder of Happy Science University and Happy Science Academy (Junior and Senior High School), Founder and President of the Happiness Realization Party, Founder and Honorary Headmaster of Happy Science Institute of Government and Management, Founder of IRH Press Co., Ltd., and the Chairperson of NEW STAR PRODUCTION Co., Ltd. and ARI Production Co., Ltd.

WHAT IS EL CANTARE?

El Cantare means "the Light of the Earth," and is the Supreme God of the Earth who has been guiding humankind since the beginning of Genesis. He is whom Jesus called Father and Muhammad called Allah, and is *Ame-no-Mioya-Gami*, Japanese Father God. Different parts of El Cantare's core consciousness have descended to Earth in the past, once as Alpha and another as Elohim. His branch spirits, such as Shakyamuni Buddha and Hermes, have descended to Earth many times and helped to flourish many civilizations. To unite various religions and to integrate various fields of study in order to build a new civilization on Earth, a part of the core consciousness has descended to Earth as Master Ryuho Okawa.

Alpha is a part of the core consciousness of El Cantare who descended to Earth around 330 million years ago. Alpha preached Earth's Truths to harmonize and unify Earth-born humans and space people who came from other planets.

Elohim is a part of El Cantare's core consciousness who descended to Earth around 150 million years ago. He gave wisdom, mainly on the differences of light and darkness, good and evil.

Ame-no-Mioya-Gami (Japanese Father God) is the Creator God and the Father God who appears in the ancient literature, *Hotsuma Tsutae*. It is believed that He descended on the foothills of Mt. Fuji about 30,000 years ago and built the Fuji dynasty, which is the root of the Japanese civilization. With justice as the central pillar, Ame-no-Mioya-Gami's teachings spread to ancient civilizations of other countries in the world.

Shakyamuni Buddha was born as a prince into the Shakya Clan in India around 2,600 years ago. When he was 29 years old, he renounced the world and sought enlightenment. He later attained Great Enlightenment and founded Buddhism.

Hermes is one of the 12 Olympian gods in Greek mythology, but the spiritual Truth is that he taught the teachings of love and progress around 4,300 years ago that became the origin of the current Western civilization. He is a hero that truly existed.

Ophealis was born in Greece around 6,500 years ago and was the leader who took an expedition to as far as Egypt. He is the God of miracles, prosperity, and arts, and is known as Osiris in the Egyptian mythology.

Rient Arl Croud was born as a king of the ancient Incan Empire around 7,000 years ago and taught about the mysteries of the mind. In the heavenly world, he is responsible for the interactions that take place between various planets.

Thoth was an almighty leader who built the golden age of the Atlantic civilization around 12,000 years ago. In the Egyptian mythology, he is known as god Thoth.

Ra Mu was a leader who built the golden age of the civilization of Mu around 17,000 years ago. As a religious leader and a politician, he ruled by uniting religion and politics.

WHAT IS A SPIRITUAL MESSAGE?

We are all spiritual beings living on this earth. The following is the mechanism behind Master Ryuho Okawa's spiritual messages.

1 You are a spirit

People are born into this world to gain wisdom through various experiences and return to the other world when their lives end. We are all spirits and repeat this cycle in order to refine our souls.

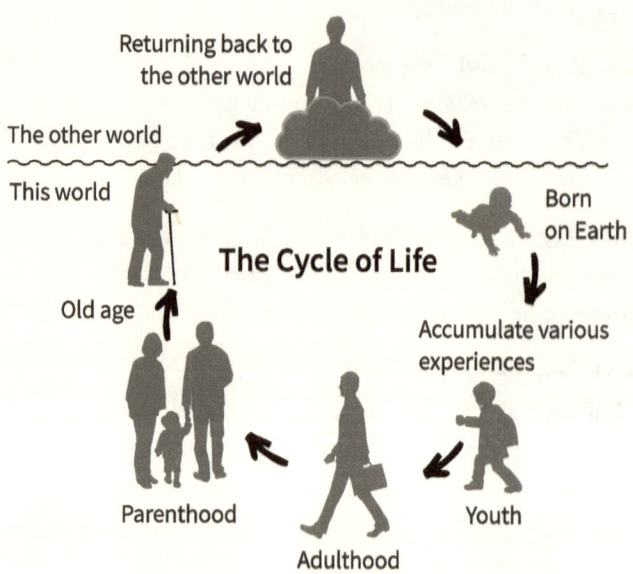

Returning back to the other world

The other world

This world

Born on Earth

The Cycle of Life

Old age

Accumulate various experiences

Parenthood

Adulthood

Youth

2 You have a guardian spirit

Guardian spirits are those who protect the people who are living on this earth. Each of us has a guardian spirit that watches over us and guides us from the other world. They were us in our past life, and are identical in how we think.

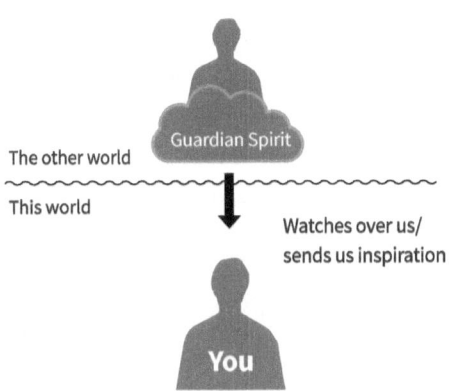

3 How spiritual messages work

Master Ryuho Okawa, through his enlightenment, is capable of summoning any spirit from anywhere in the world, including the spirit world.

Master Okawa's way of receiving spiritual messages is fundamentally different from that of other psychic mediums who undergo trances and are thereby completely taken over by the spirits they are channeling.

Master Okawa's attainment of a high level of enlightenment enables him to retain full control of his consciousness and body throughout the duration of the spiritual message. To allow the spirits to express their own thoughts and personalities freely, however, Master Okawa usually softens the dominancy of his consciousness. This way, he is able to keep his own philosophies out of the way and ensure that the spiritual messages are pure expressions of the spirits he is channeling.

Since guardian spirits think at the same subconscious level as the person living on earth, Master Okawa can summon the spirit and find out what the person on earth is actually thinking. If the person has already returned to the other world, the spirit can give messages to the people living on earth through Master Okawa.

Since 2009, many spiritual messages have been openly recorded by Master Okawa and published. Spiritual messages from the guardian spirits of people living today such as Donald Trump, former Japanese Prime Minister Shinzo Abe and Chinese President Xi Jinping, as well as spiritual messages sent from the spirit world by Jesus Christ, Muhammad, Thomas Edison, Mother Teresa, Steve Jobs and Nelson Mandela are just a tiny pack of spiritual messages that were published so far.

Domestically, in Japan, these spiritual messages are being read by a wide range of politicians and mass media, and the high-level contents of these books are delivering an impact even more on politics, news and public opinion. In recent years, there have been spiritual messages recorded in English, and

English translations are being done on the spiritual messages given in Japanese. These have been published overseas, one after another, and have started to shake the world.

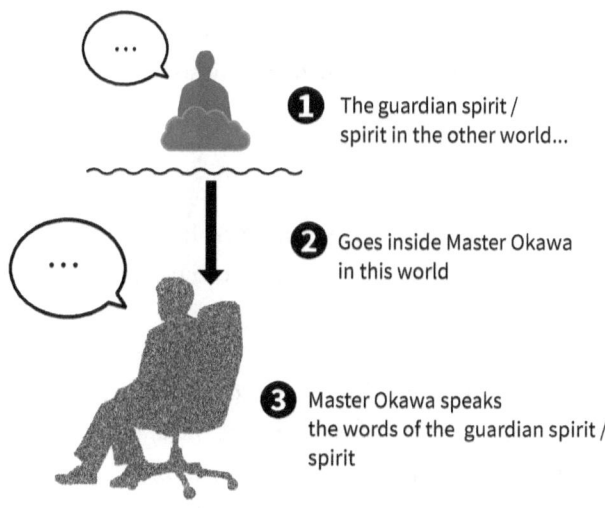

1. The guardian spirit / spirit in the other world...

2. Goes inside Master Okawa in this world

3. Master Okawa speaks the words of the guardian spirit / spirit

For more about spiritual messages and a complete list of books in the Spiritual Interview Series, visit okawabooks.com

ABOUT HAPPY SCIENCE

Happy Science is a global movement that empowers individuals to find purpose and spiritual happiness and to share that happiness with their families, societies, and the world. With more than 12 million members around the world, Happy Science aims to increase awareness of spiritual truths and expand our capacity for love, compassion, and joy so that together we can create the kind of world we all wish to live in.

Activities at Happy Science are based on the Principle of Happiness (Love, Wisdom, Self-Reflection, and Progress). This principle embraces worldwide philosophies and beliefs, transcending boundaries of culture and religions.

Love teaches us to give ourselves freely without expecting anything in return; it encompasses giving, nurturing, and forgiving.

Wisdom leads us to the insights of spiritual truths, and opens us to the true meaning of life and the will of God (the universe, the highest power, Buddha).

Self-Reflection brings a mindful, nonjudgmental lens to our thoughts and actions to help us find our truest selves—the essence of our souls—and deepen our connection to the highest power. It helps us attain a clean and peaceful mind and leads us to the right life path.

Progress emphasizes the positive, dynamic aspects of our spiritual growth—actions we can take to manifest and spread happiness around the world. It's a path that not only expands our soul growth, but also furthers the collective potential of the world we live in.

PROGRAMS AND EVENTS

The doors of Happy Science are open to all. We offer a variety of programs and events, including self-exploration and self-growth programs, spiritual seminars, meditation and contemplation sessions, study groups, and book events.

Our programs are designed to:
* Deepen your understanding of your purpose and meaning in life
* Improve your relationships and increase your capacity to love unconditionally
* Attain peace of mind, decrease anxiety and stress, and feel positive
* Gain deeper insights and a broader perspective on the world
* Learn how to overcome life's challenges
  ... and much more.

For more information, visit happy-science.org.

OUR ACTIVITIES

Happy Science does other various activities to provide support for those in need.

◆ **You Are An Angel! General Incorporated Association**

Happy Science has a volunteer network in Japan that encourages and supports children with disabilities as well as their parents and guardians.

◆ **Never Mind School for Truancy**

At 'Never Mind,' we support students who find it very challenging to attend schools in Japan. We also nurture their self-help spirit and power to rebound against obstacles in life based on Master Okawa's teachings and faith.

◆ **"Prevention Against Suicide" Campaign since 2003**

A nationwide campaign to reduce suicides; over 20,000 people commit suicide every year in Japan. "The Suicide Prevention Website-Words of Truth for You-" presents spiritual prescriptions for worries such as depression, lost love, extramarital affairs, bullying and work-related problems, thereby saving many lives.

◆ **Support for Anti-bullying Campaigns**

Happy Science provides support for a group of parents and guardians, Network to Protect Children from Bullying, a general incorporated foundation launched in Japan to end bullying, including those that can even be called a criminal offense. So far, the network received more than 5,000 cases and resolved 90% of them.

- **The Golden Age Scholarship**

  This scholarship is granted to students who can contribute greatly and bring a hopeful future to the world.

- **Success No.1**

  Buddha's Truth Afterschool Academy

  Happy Science has over 180 classrooms throughout Japan and in several cities around the world that focus on afterschool education for children. The education focuses on faith and morals in addition to supporting children's school studies.

- **Angel Plan V**

  For children under the age of kindergarten, Happy Science holds classes for nurturing healthy, positive, and creative boys and girls.

- **Future Stars Training Department**

  The Future Stars Training Department was founded within the Happy Science Media Division with the goal of nurturing talented individuals to become successful in the performing arts and entertainment industry.

- **NEW STAR PRODUCTION Co., Ltd.**

  ARI Production Co., Ltd.

  We have companies to nurture actors and actresses, artists, and vocalists. They are also involved in film production.

CONTACT INFORMATION

Happy Science is a worldwide organization with branches and temples around the globe. For a comprehensive list, visit the worldwide directory at *happy-science.org*. The following are some of the many Happy Science locations:

UNITED STATES AND CANADA

New York
79 Franklin St., New York, NY 10013, USA
Phone: 1-212-343-7972
Fax: 1-212-343-7973
Email: ny@happy-science.org
Website: happyscience-usa.org

New Jersey
66 Hudson St., #2R, Hoboken, NJ 07030, USA
Phone: 1-201-313-0127
Email: nj@happy-science.org
Website: happyscience-usa.org

Chicago
2300 Barrington Rd., Suite #400,
Hoffman Estates, IL 60169, USA
Phone: 1-630-937-3077
Email: chicago@happy-science.org
Website: happyscience-usa.org

Florida
5208 8th St., Zephyrhills, FL 33542, USA
Phone: 1-813-715-0000
Fax: 1-813-715-0010
Email: florida@happy-science.org
Website: happyscience-usa.org

Atlanta
1874 Piedmont Ave., NE Suite 360-C
Atlanta, GA 30324, USA
Phone: 1-404-892-7770
Email: atlanta@happy-science.org
Website: happyscience-usa.org

San Francisco
525 Clinton St.
Redwood City, CA 94062, USA
Phone & Fax: 1-650-363-2777
Email: sf@happy-science.org
Website: happyscience-usa.org

Los Angeles
1590 E. Del Mar Blvd., Pasadena, CA
91106, USA
Phone: 1-626-395-7775
Fax: 1-626-395-7776
Email: la@happy-science.org
Website: happyscience-usa.org

Orange County
16541 Gothard St. Suite 104
Huntington Beach, CA 92647
Phone: 1-714-659-1501
Email: oc@happy-science.org
Website: happyscience-usa.org

San Diego
7841 Balboa Ave. Suite #202
San Diego, CA 92111, USA
Phone: 1-626-395-7775
Fax: 1-626-395-7776
E-mail: sandiego@happy-science.org
Website: happyscience-usa.org

Hawaii
Phone: 1-808-591-9772
Fax: 1-808-591-9776
Email: hi@happy-science.org
Website: happyscience-usa.org

Kauai
3343 Kanakolu Street, Suite 5
Lihue, HI 96766, USA
Phone: 1-808-822-7007
Fax: 1-808-822-6007
Email: kauai-hi@happy-science.org
Website: happyscience-usa.org

Toronto

845 The Queensway
Etobicoke, ON M8Z 1N6, Canada
Phone: 1-416-901-3747
Email: toronto@happy-science.org
Website: happy-science.ca

Vancouver

#201-2607 East 49th Avenue,
Vancouver, BC, V5S 1J9, Canada
Phone: 1-604-437-7735
Fax: 1-604-437-7764
Email: vancouver@happy-science.org
Website: happy-science.ca

INTERNATIONAL

Tokyo

1-6-7 Togoshi, Shinagawa,
Tokyo, 142-0041, Japan
Phone: 81-3-6384-5770
Fax: 81-3-6384-5776
Email: tokyo@happy-science.org
Website: happy-science.org

Seoul

74, Sadang-ro 27-gil,
Dongjak-gu, Seoul, Korea
Phone: 82-2-3478-8777
Fax: 82-2-3478-9777
Email: korea@happy-science.org
Website: happyscience-korea.org

London

3 Margaret St.
London, W1W 8RE United Kingdom
Phone: 44-20-7323-9255
Fax: 44-20-7323-9344
Email: eu@happy-science.org
Website: www.happyscience-uk.org

Taipei

No. 89, Lane 155, Dunhua N. Road,
Songshan District, Taipei City 105, Taiwan
Phone: 886-2-2719-9377
Fax: 886-2-2719-5570
Email: taiwan@happy-science.org
Website: happyscience-tw.org

Sydney

516 Pacific Highway, Lane Cove North,
2066 NSW, Australia
Phone: 61-2-9411-2877
Fax: 61-2-9411-2822
Email: sydney@happy-science.org

Kuala Lumpur

No 22A, Block 2, Jalil Link Jalan Jalil
Jaya 2, Bukit Jalil 57000,
Kuala Lumpur, Malaysia
Phone: 60-3-8998-7877
Fax: 60-3-8998-7977
Email: malaysia@happy-science.org
Website: happyscience.org.my

Sao Paulo

Rua. Domingos de Morais 1154,
Vila Mariana, Sao Paulo SP
CEP 04010-100, Brazil
Phone: 55-11-5088-3800
Email: sp@happy-science.org
Website: happyscience.com.br

Kathmandu

Kathmandu Metropolitan City,
Ward No. 15, Ring Road, Kimdol,
Sitapaila Kathmandu, Nepal
Phone: 977-1-427-2931
Email: nepal@happy-science.org

Jundiai

Rua Congo, 447, Jd. Bonfiglioli
Jundiai-CEP, 13207-340, Brazil
Phone: 55-11-4587-5952
Email: jundiai@happy-science.org

Kampala

Plot 877 Rubaga Road, Kampala
P.O. Box 34130 Kampala, UGANDA
Email: uganda@happy-science.org

ABOUT HAPPINESS REALIZATION PARTY

The Happiness Realization Party (HRP) was founded in May 2009 by Master Ryuho Okawa as part of the Happy Science Group. HRP strives to improve the Japanese society, based on three basic political principles of "freedom, democracy, and faith," and let Japan promote individual and public happiness from Asia to the world as a leader nation.

1) Diplomacy and Security: Protecting Freedom, Democracy, and Faith of Japan and the World from China's Totalitarianism

Japan's current defense system is insufficient against China's expanding hegemony and the threat of North Korea's nuclear missiles. Japan, as the leader of Asia, must strengthen its defense power and promote strategic diplomacy together with the nations which share the values of freedom, democracy, and faith. Further, HRP aims to realize world peace under the leadership of Japan, the nation with the spirit of religious tolerance.

2) Economy: Early economic recovery through utilizing the "wisdom of the private sector"

Economy has been damaged severely by the novel coronavirus originated in China. Many companies have been forced into bankruptcy or out of business. What is needed for economic recovery now is not subsidies and regulations by the government, but policies which can utilize the "wisdom of the private sector."

For more information, visit en.hr-party.jp

HAPPY SCIENCE ACADEMY
JUNIOR AND SENIOR HIGH SCHOOL

Happy Science Academy Junior and Senior High School is a boarding school founded with the goal of educating the future leaders of the world who can have a big vision, persevere, and take on new challenges.

Currently, there are two campuses in Japan; the Nasu Main Campus in Tochigi Prefecture, founded in 2010, and the Kansai Campus in Shiga Prefecture, founded in 2013.

Nasu Main Campus

Kansai Campus

 **HAPPY SCIENCE UNIVERSITY**

THE FOUNDING SPIRIT AND THE GOAL OF EDUCATION

Based on the founding philosophy of the university, "Exploration of happiness and the creation of a new civilization," education, research and studies will be provided to help students acquire deep understanding grounded in religious belief and advanced expertise with the objectives of producing "great talents of virtue" who can contribute in a broad-ranging way to serve Japan and the international society.

FACULTIES

Faculty of human happiness

Students in this faculty will pursue liberal arts from various perspectives with a multidisciplinary approach, explore and envision an ideal state of human beings and society.

Faculty of successful management

This faculty aims to realize successful management that helps organizations to create value and wealth for society and to contribute to the happiness and the development of management and employees as well as society as a whole.

Faculty of future creation

Students in this faculty study subjects such as political science, journalism, performing arts and artistic expression, and explore and present new political and cultural models based on truth, goodness and beauty.

Faculty of future industry

This faculty aims to nurture engineers who can resolve various issues facing modern civilization from a technological standpoint and contribute to the creation of new industries of the future.

ABOUT HS PRESS

HS Press is an imprint of IRH Press Co., Ltd. IRH Press Co., Ltd., based in Tokyo, was founded in 1987 as a publishing division of Happy Science. IRH Press publishes religious and spiritual books, journals, magazines and also operates broadcast and film production enterprises. For more information, visit *okawabooks.com*.

Follow us on:

f Facebook: Okawa Books   **◎** Instagram: OkawaBooks

▶ Youtube: Okawa Books   **🐦** Twitter: Okawa Books

𝓟 Pinterest: Okawa Books   **g** Goodreads: Ryuho Okawa

--------- **NEWSLETTER** ---------

To receive book related news, promotions and events, please subscribe to our newsletter below.

𝜌 eepurl.com/bsMeJj

 --------- **AUDIO / VISUAL MEDIA** ---------

YOUTUBE

PODCAST

Introduction of Ryuho Okawa's titles; topics ranging from self-help, current affairs, spirituality, religion, and the universe.

BOOKS BY RYUHO OKAWA

RYUHO OKAWA'S LAWS SERIES

The Laws Series is an annual volume of books that are comprised of Ryuho Okawa's lectures that function as universal guidance to all people. They are of various topics that were given in accordance with the changes that each year brings. *The Laws of the Sun*, the first publication of the laws series, ranked in the annual best-selling list in Japan in 1994. Since, the laws series' titles have ranked in the annual best-selling list every year for more than two decades, setting socio-cultural trends in Japan and around the world.

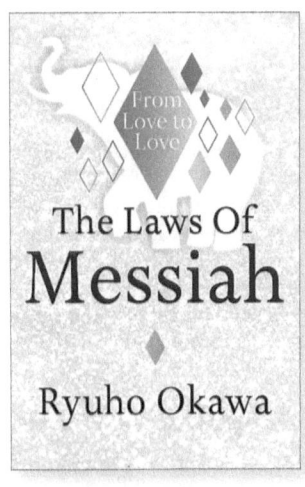

The 28th Laws Series
The Laws Of Messiah

From Love to Love

Paperback • 248 pages • $16.95
ISBN: 978-1-942125-90-7 (Jan. 31, 2022)

"What is Messiah?" This book carries an important message of love and guidance to people living now from the Modern-Day Messiah or the Modern-Day Savior. It also reveals the secret of Shambhala, the spiritual center of Earth, as well as the truth that this spiritual center is currently in danger of perishing and what we can do to protect this sacred place.

Love your Lord God. Know that those who don't know love don't know God. Discover the true love of God and the ideal practice of faith. This book teaches the most important element we must not lose sight of as we go through our soul training on this planet Earth.

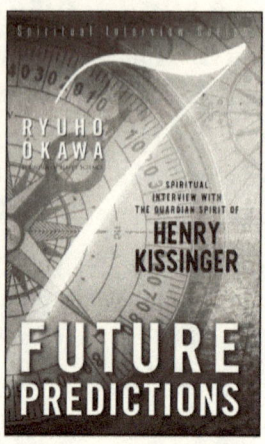

7 Future Predictions
Spiritual Interview with the Guardian Spirit of Henry Kissinger

Henry Kissinger is an expert in international politics who served as the U.S. secretary of state for both Nixon and Ford administrations,. In this book, his guardian spirit (a part of Kissinger's subconscious) makes seven near-future predictions (as of September 2016) including political issues in the U.S. that could occur as a result of the presidential election, as well as the future of the EU, Islamic countries, China and North Korea.

Spiritual Interview with George Washington

Revealing Donald Trump's Hidden Identity

What would George Washington say about today's America?
Read this and find out! America's Founding Father's current thoughts on Racial problems, America's foreign policies, The American and world economies, and his mission and the secret of his soul.

THE TRUMP SECRET

SEEING THROUGH THE PAST, PRESENT, AND FUTURE OF THE NEW AMERICAN PRESIDENT

This book contains a series of lectures and interviews that unveil the secrets to Trump's victory and makes predictions of what will happen under his presidency. This book predicts the coming of a new America that will go through a great transformation from the "red and blue states" to the United States.

A NEW MESSAGE FROM BARACK OBAMA

INTERVIEWING THE GUARDIAN SPIRIT OF THE PRESIDENT OF THE UNITED STATES

This spiritual interview reveals President Obama's stance on international relations. Now that America is "on the verge of crisis," as the guardian spirit of President Obama says in this interview, we all need to think about how we can achieve security, justice and peace in the world without the "world's policeman."

PUTIN'S INSIGHTS ON RUSSIA, JAPAN AND THE WORLD

AN INTERVIEW WITH THE GUARDIAN SPIRIT OF THE PRESIDENT OF RUSSIA

In this book, Master Ryuho Okawa summons the guardian spirit of President Putin and asks his opinion on the current world leaders, how he looks upon Syrian affairs and the confusion in the EU, and on what he predicts will happen in the next 5 years with the Asian crisis.

INTO THE STORM OF INTERNATIONAL POLITICS

THE NEW STANDARDS OF THE WORLD ORDER

The world is now seeking a new idea or a new philosophy that will show the countries with such values the direction they should head in. In this book, Okawa presents new standards of the world order while giving his own analysis on world affairs concerning the U.S., China, Islamic State and others.

RYUHO OKAWA - A POLITICAL REVOLUTIONARY

THE ORIGINATOR OF ABENOMICS AND FATHER OF THE HAPPINESS REALIZATION PARTY

In this book, the Founder and the Master of Happy Science Group as well as the Father of Happiness Realization Party, Master Okawa lays down the guiding principles and the ways to breakthrough on the topics of economy, finance, nuclear power plant, foreign diplomacy, social welfare, and society with aging population and a falling birth rate.

THE IMPORTANCE OF THE EXPLORATION OF THE RIGHT MIND

The basic teaching of Happy Science is 'the exploration of the Right Mind.' The significance of this book is in that it covers the exploration of the Right Mind for the citizen based on a macro-perspective understanding, with whom true sovereignty lies, in addition to the way to explore the Right Mind for the individual religious practitioner.

HAVE FAITH IN GREAT AMERICA

LIBERTY AND WORLD JUSTICE FOR ALL

This book is Master Ryuho Okawa's earnest message to the United States of America. The world's future depends on America's fulfillment of its long-held sacred mission of protecting the faith, liberty, and justice of people and nations around the world, and on the development of strong bonds between the United States and Japan.

THE MANIFESTO OF THE HAPPINESS REALIZATION PARTY

This book is a historical declaration to change the world through a peaceful revolution by the philosophy and speech based on the Truth, rather than by violence or massacre. It also states on the assessment of the meaning of WWII as well as how the relation between religion and politics should be. It is a must read for all people who wish to build a true utopia.

THE POWER TO LEAD THE WORLD

"It is not enough to speak only of ideals; we must envision how this world should be while setting our eyes firmly on things like real politics."

—Master Ryuho Okawa

[This book is available only in local branches and temples. Please refer to the contact information.]

THE LAWS OF THE SUN

ONE SOURCE, ONE PLANET, ONE PEOPLE

Imagine if you could ask God why He created this world and what spiritual laws He used to shape us—and everything around us. If we could understand His designs and intentions, we could discover what our goals in life should be and whether our actions move us closer to those goals or farther away.

THE GOLDEN LAWS

HISTORY THROUGH THE EYES OF THE ETERNAL BUDDHA

The Golden Laws reveals how Buddha's Plan has been unfolding on earth, and outlines five thousand years of the secret history of humankind. Once we understand the true course of history, we cannot help but become aware of the significance of our spiritual mission in the present age.

THE NINE DIMENSIONS

UNVEILING THE LAWS OF ETERNITY

This book is a window into the mind of our loving God, who encourages us to grow into greater angels. It reveals His deepest intentions, answering the timely question of why He conceived such a colorful medley of religions, philosophies, sciences, arts, and other forms of expression.

A NEW MESSAGE FROM VLADIMIR PUTIN

INVERVIEWING THE GUARDIAN SPIRIT OF THE PRESIDENT OF RUSSIA

We hereby bring you the spiritual message from the guardian spirit of President Putin, the politician who is the center of attention of not just the people of Russia but of the whole world, regardless of it being in a good or a bad way. In the Preface, it says, "President Putin's true intentions, which are 90 percent misunderstood."

PRESIDENT PUTIN AND THE FUTURE OF RUSSIA

AN INTERVIEW WITH THE GUARDIAN SPIRIT OF VLADIMIR PUTIN

"I have no intention of fighting the United States. The Cold War is over... I have no intention of fighting the Americans... And I'm not friendly enough with China to think about joining them against the United States... I have given Russians religious freedom, which makes me very different from the Chinese."

—Putin's Guardian Spirit

CHINA'S HIDDEN AGENDA

THE MASTERMIND BEHIND THE ANTI-AMERICAN AND ANTI-JAPANESE PROTESTS

"I wanted to stir up the anti-American movement in the Arab world to make sure that the United States won't be able to attack Syria or Iran...I'm the mastermind behind the Muhammad video."

—Xi Jinping's Guardian Spirit

134

INTERVIEWING THE GUARDIAN SPIRIT OF U.S AMBASSADOR CAROLINE KENNEDY

A NEW BRIDGE BETWEEN JAPAN AND THE U.S.

What is Ambassador Kennedy's views on Japan-U. S. and Japan-China relations? How does she view World War II? What was the reason behind the Kennedy tragedies? What does she seek from the Japanese and American people? Find the answers in this book.

WAS DROPPING THE ATOMIC BOMBS A CRIME AGAINST HUMANITY?

INSIGHTS FROM HARRY S. TRUMAN AND FRANKLIN D. ROOSEVELT

Was there any true justification for the atomic bombing? To answer to this question, Master Ryuho Okawa conducted spiritual interviews with Truman and Roosevelt. This book reveals valuable information that will help the world gain a truthful understanding of world history.

THE TRUTH OF THE PACIFIC WAR

SOULFUL MESSAGES FROM HIDEKI TOJO, JAPAN'S WARTIME LEADER INCLUDING A SPIRITUAL INTERVIEW WITH GENERAL DOUGLAS MACARTHUR

The material provided is a testimony by General Hideki Tojo, who was Japan's most significant figure in the Pacific War. Furthermore, we have also recorded a testimony by Supreme Commander of the Allied Powers Douglas MacArthur in order to ensure a fair argument.

ARE ISLAMIC EXTREMISTS JIHADISTS OR TERRORISTS?

THE NECESSITY OF FREEDOM IN ISLAMIC COUNTRIES

"As the world teacher, it was my duty to determine from a religious perspective whether it is true that the militant Islamic extremists are terrorist organizations, as the West calls them, or whether we should accept them as jihadists of pure faith. I found the answer in this interview."

-From Afterword

THE JUST CAUSE IN THE IRAQ WAR

DID SADDAM HUSSEIN POSSESS WEAPONS OF MASS DESTRUCTION?

In this book, you will discover that Saddam Hussein was also behind the planning of the 9/11 terrorist attacks and both he and Osama bin Laden are now in Hell. The knowledge this book provides will help each of us make the right decisions as we work together to create a peaceful international society.

A SPIRITUAL INTERVIEW WITH THE LEADER OF ISIL, AL-BAGHDADI

INCLUDING SPIRITUAL INVESTIGATION INTO THE TRUTH OF THE JAPANESE HOSTAGE TAKING

The author believes we must see through the destiny of ISIL from the viewpoint of world history. Terrorism must not be tolerated, of course—but this book is a precious source to see ISIL in an objective and impartial way.

THE SYRIAN CRISIS

WHAT IS GOD'S VERDICT ON U.S. MILITARY INTERVENTION?

As this interview reveals, the Syrian dictator's true character is quite different from what we saw in the CBS interview. As the world braces for a possible world war, Master Ryuho Okawa provides us with a clear sense of where God's justice lies in this international crisis.

EXPOSING NORTH KOREA'S MENACING LEADER

KIM JONG UN'S PLOT FOR A PSYCHOLOGICAL WAR

This book reveals the role that North Korea is playing in China's imperialistic strategy and the two nations' close ties with Iran. Together, China and Kim Jong Un are carrying out a psychological war that takes full advantage of the weaknesses of Japanese Prime Minister Abe and United States President Obama.

UNMASKING BAN KI-MOON'S BIASED STANCE

INVESTIGATING THE PARALYSIS OF THE UNITED NATIONS

Can we depend on Ban Ki-moon to successfully uphold the principle of impartiality in the United Nations's role of peacemaking? In this spiritual interview, Master Okawa reveals the U.N. Secretary-General's true character and true intentions regarding his important peacemaking responsibilities.

Messages From Heaven
What Jesus, Buddha, Muhammad, and Moses Would Say Today

If you could speak to Jesus, Buddha, Moses, or Muhammad, what would you ask? In this book, Ryuho Okawa shares the spiritual communication he had with these four spirits and the messages they want to share with people living today. The Truths revealed in this book will open your eyes to a level of spiritual awareness, salvation, and happiness that you have never experienced before.

Think Big!
Be Positive and Be Brave to Achieve Your Dreams

Think Big! offers the support and encouragement to shift to new ways of thinking and mastering self-discipline. Okawa's self-proven approach fosters stability and strength in the challenges each of us faces. In addition to his relatable stories and a motivational voice to keep us going, each chapter builds on the next for concrete methodologies that, when added up, are a track to support your dreams, yourself, and your life.

The Heart of Work
10 Keys to Living Your Calling

In this book, Ryuho Okawa shares 10 key philosophies and goals to live by to guide us through our work lives and triumphantly live our calling. There are key principles that will help you get to the heart of work, manage your time well, prioritize your work, live with long health and vitality, achieve growth, and more.

THE MIRACLE OF MEDITATION
OPENING YOUR LIFE TO PEACE, JOY, AND THE POWER WITHIN

This book introduces various types of meditation, including calming meditation, purposeful meditation, reading meditation, reflective meditation, and meditation to communicate with heaven. Through reading and practicing meditation in this book, we can experience the miracle of meditation, which is to start living a life of peace, happiness, and success.

THE ESSENCE OF BUDDHA
THE PATH TO ENLIGHTENMENT

This book is about living a life with meaning and purpose. It offers a contemporary interpretation of the way to enlightenment, written by highly revered spiritual leader. The fundamental tenets of the Buddhist understanding of life, such as The Eightfold Path, The Six Paramitas and the Laws of Causality, are clearly explained in modern and accessible terms, along with the need for self-reflection, the nature of karma and reincarnation, and other teachings of the Buddha. Enlightenment is a potential achievement for every sentient being

THE REBIRTH OF BUDDHA
MY ETERNAL DISCIPLES, HEAR MY WORDS

These are the messages of Buddha who has returned to this modern age as promised to His eternal beloved disciples. They are in simple words and poetic style, yet contain profound messages. Once you start reading these passages, your soul will be replenished as the plant absorbs the water, and you will remember why you chose this era to be born into with Buddha. Listen to the voices of your Eternal Master and awaken to your calling.

MUSIC BY RYUHO OKAWA

El Cantare Ryuho Okawa Original Songs

A song celebrating Lord God

A song celebrating Lord God,
the God of the Earth,
who is beyond a prophet.

DVD
CD

The Water Revolution

English and Chinese version

For the truth and happiness of
the 1.4 billion people in China
who have no freedom. Love,
justice, and sacred rage of God
are on this melody that will
give you courage to fight to
bring peace.

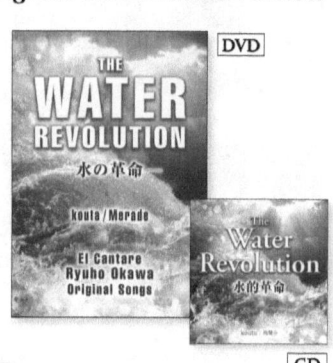

DVD

CD

Search on YouTube

the water revolution for a short ad!

Listen now today!

With Savior *English version*

This is the message of hope to the modern people who are living in the midst of the Coronavirus pandemic, natural disasters, economic depression, and other various crises.

Search on YouTube

with savior for a short ad!

The Thunder
a composition for repelling the Coronavirus

We have been granted this music from our Lord. It will repel away the novel Coronavirus originated in China. Experience this magnificent powerful music.

Search on YouTube

the thunder composition

for a short ad!

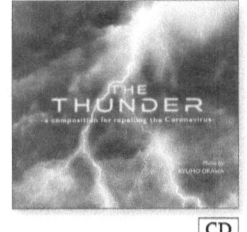

The Exorcism
prayer music for repelling Lost Spirits

Feel the divine vibrations of this Japanese and Western exorcising symphony to banish all evil possessions you suffer from and to purify your space!

Search on YouTube

the exorcism repelling

for a short ad!